For Luke

First paperback edition 1997

A CIP catalogue record for this book is available
from the British Library.
ISBN 0-7136-4787-6

First published 1990 in hardback by A & C Black (Publishers) Ltd, 35 Bedford Row, London WC1R 4JH
© 1990, 1997 A & C Black (Publishers) Ltd

Photographs © 1990, 1997 Fiona Pragoff
except page 20, S.& O Matthews

Acknowledgements
Edited by Barbara Taylor
Science consultant Dr Bryson Gore
Illustrations by Alex Ayliffe

The photographer, authors and publishers would like
to thank the following people whose help and
co-operation made this book possible:
Crystal, Emily, Simon and their parents.
The staff and pupils at St George's School.

Typeset by Spectrum Typesetting, London
Printed in Singapore by Tien Wah Press (Pte.) Ltd

My Jumper

Robert Pressling
Photographs by Fiona Pragoff

A & C Black · London

Look at all the colours and patterns on these jumpers. Which one do you like best?

This is my favourite jumper.

On the label, there's a special picture.
It means my jumper is made from wool.

When I pull on my jumper,
it feels soft and warm.

5

The pattern goes right round my jumper.

6

The pattern outside my jumper...

...is different from the pattern
inside my jumper.

My jumper can stretch. If Emily lets go, what will happen?

My jumper is full of little holes.
I can see through my jumper.

On the cuffs of my jumper, there are lots of loops.

Simon is knitting a jumper.

Can you see how he loops the wool around the needles?

Oops! I've spilt some ice-cream.
My jumper needs a wash.

Simon and Emily are helping me to wash my jumper.

Look at all the bubbles!

15

My jumper soaks
up the water.
It feels heavy.

But if I squeeze out the water,
my jumper feels lighter.

Tomorrow, we're going to a farm.

I'm going to wear my clean jumper.

This wool comes from a sheep.

It looks and feels different from the wool in my jumper.

Look at all these wools. How many differences can you spot?

This is just like the wool in my jumper.

More things to do

1. Wool and other fibres
Wool is a very special sort of fibre. Compare it with other fibres, such as cotton, silk and nylon. Look at the fibres with a magnifying glass and investigate the weight, feel, stretchiness and strength of each fibre. How far will each fibre stretch before it breaks? Try pulling out a long thread of sheep's wool. Can you twist this to make a strong piece of yarn? Wool shrinks in hot water. Does this happen to other fibres? Which fibres are best at keeping things warm or cool?

2. Washing wool
See if you can work out the best conditions for washing wool. How can you make a dirt smudge of the same size on each piece of wool? You can change things such as the temperature of the water, the type and amount of soap powder and the number of rubs or squeezes. Is it easier to clean the wool if you leave it to soak first?

3. Symbols and signs
See if you can think of any other symbols like the woolmark, which are used all over the world. How long can you make your list?

4. Design a pattern
Can you design a pattern for a jumper? Use squared paper and different coloured pencils. Each square stands for one stitch. Mark a coloured cross in each square to show the colour you want each stitch to be. You could design a pattern with animals, trains or your favourite toy.

Find the page

This list shows you where to find some of the ideas in this book.

Notes for parents and teachers

As you share this book with young children, these notes will help you to explain the scientific concepts behind the different activities.

Pages 2, 3, 6, 7   Colours and patterns

Jumpers can be sorted into different groups according to their colour or pattern. Patterns with a mixture of colours are made by carrying each colour along the back of the jumper and joining it into the knitting each time it is needed.

Page 4   Labels on jumpers

This symbol is the International Wool Secretariat's symbol for products made from pure new wool. It is called the woolmark. The same symbol is used all over the world on clothes, carpets, curtains and blankets.

Page 5   How warm are jumpers?

Wool traps a dry layer of air which helps to hold in body heat and keep us warm. This ability to stop heat escaping is called insulation.

Pages 8, 9   Stretching jumpers

Wool fibres are so flexible, they can be bent and twisted again and again without breaking. A wool fibre can be stretched up to 40 per cent beyond its original length before it breaks. This makes wool very difficult to tear. The fibres have a natural waviness, called crimp, which makes the fibres spring back into shape after they have been stretched.

Pages 10, 11   Knitting jumpers

A good way to see how knitting works is to find an old woollen jumper and pull it apart to show how the wool is looped together in stitches. The loops on the cuffs of a jumper show where the wool was cast on to make the first row of loops.

Pages 13, 14, 15, 18, 19   Washing jumpers

The soap breaks down the surface tension of the water so it forms smaller droplets and flows into all the places where dirt is trapped. The soap also surrounds the particles of dirt and makes them float off into the water so they can be rinsed away. If the water is too hot, the wool will shrink.

Pages 16, 17   Wet jumpers

On the surface, a wool fibre has overlapping scales (like tiny roof tiles) which repel liquid. But the inner core of the fibre absorbs moisture. So a small amount of water will run off the surface of a woollen jumper. But if the wool gets really wet (as it does when it's washed), it soaks up a lot of water and becomes very heavy.

Pages 20, 21   Wool from sheep

The wool from a sheep has to be processed before it can be used to knit jumpers. It is washed, dyed, carded (untangled), rolled into a sausage shape called a rolag or sliver and finally spun into yarn. See if the children can find out more about all the different stages in processing wool.

Pages 22, 23   All sorts of wool

The wool in the shops comes in different thicknesses, such as four-ply and double knitting.

Most wool comes from sheep but fluffy mohair wool comes from a goat and angora wool comes from a rabbit.

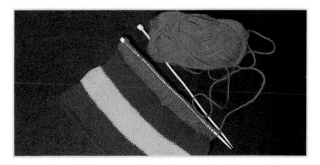